Daniel Poppick is "assisted by a rad[...] [...]l lines show grammar almost breaking up: For you was s[...] [...]m buoyed by / Homages…" Bending, buoyancy—the poems have both delicacy and force. "We am" might be a solecism, but it's also an urgent dream. Reading, we am radiant. "Between us flows a school."

BEN LERNER (CITATION FOR THE *BOMB* BIENNIAL POETRY PRIZE)

With mesmerizing dexterity, Daniel Poppick captures a consciousness hived by the augmented realities of contemporary life. As distance collapses into sharable moments, he questions how we can sustain intimacy when we cease distinguishing our somatic experiences from our avatars; how to disrupt when disruption itself is privatized; how to connect when connection itself is privatized? Each poem reads like exquisite comment streams of the mind. Poppick writes with beauty, wit, and compassion.

CATHY PARK HONG

As you near the conclusion of Poppick's gorgeous collection, having followed the drive of his propulsive grammar through remarkably moving poems that manage wild elaboration with the bite of aphorism, you come upon a speaker, himself on the way to a poetry reading, let's call him Poppick, being pulled over by the police: "You shrugged & I, / A little alarmed / By exposure to a force / Coiled more tightly than my own / Followed him & fixed / Myself in his front seat." Poppick and the officer share a brief and official conversation about the speaker's vocation, poetry, and "I discerned a muted affection, but will never be certain / As sympathy & contempt often run the same drills / On the field of the face." This is a collection replete with the vulnerable pathos of possible connections like this one, tense with longing, and bright with tender, brilliant wit that's turned by the torque of exquisite syntax. This is one of my very favorite new collections. It reminds me why I read poems in the first place. "Remember how you once / Kissed a map / And it was cool and bottomless…"? This book is that kiss.

ROBYN SCHIFF

"Now I am older, don't think in words." Poppick's poems live up to the claim. Thinking in words might entail articulating orderly, permissible ideas. This is closer to the police's job, yet who doesn't have an inner cop? "Thus I am inwardly my police," he writes. Reminding us of how "unvarious by comparison" ordinary language is, Poppick's poetry amazes as the result of perceiving in words, full on, riotously.

MÓNICA DE LA TORRE

THE POLICE

Cover photo courtesy of the author.

Cover and interior text set in Didot, Futura Std, and Joanna MT Std

Cover and interior design by Gillian Olivia Blythe Hamel

Offset printed in the United States
by Edwards Brothers Malloy, Ann Arbor, Michigan
On 55# Enviro Natural 100% Recycled 100% PCW
Acid Free Archival Quality FSC Certified Paper

Library of Congress Cataloging-in-Publication Data

Names: Poppick, Daniel, 1985- author.
Title: The police / Daniel Poppick.
Description: Oakland, California : Omnidawn Publishing, 2017.
Identifiers: LCCN 2016045487 | ISBN 9781632430342 (pbk. : alk.
  paper)
Classification: LCC PS3616.O659 A6 2017 | DDC 811/.6--dc23
LC record available at https://lccn.loc.gov/2016045487

Published by Omnidawn Publishing, Oakland, California
www.omnidawn.com (510) 237-5472 (800) 792-4957
10 9 8 7 6 5 4 3 2 1
ISBN: 978-1-63243-034-2

THE POLICE

DANIEL POPPICK

OMNIDAWN PUBLISHING
OAKLAND, CALIFORNIA
2017

TABLE OF CONTENTS

IV.

V.

For Callie, Eric, and Margaret

CLAIRE: He's always finding the maids' hairs all over the pinks and roses!

SOLANGE: And things about our private lives with—

CLAIRE: With? With?

(Jean Genet, The Maids)

PINK STONES

Leaking from home through its existing door
Yesterday I saw this vacant stranger
Walking blasted through the street
His head's port (you couldn't call it
A face with precision) grimaced and his gait
Rose wool, which also happened to be what
He had noosed on the pile you'd call his dome
You look at him and his body just sprays
And storms each witness
As I trust when told others are an act of violence against me
How does one approach a person, do you go like "Hi"
Ambulance running it
I speak to him here through a brick-fucked window
Lit on a street these nouns infect

Carrying their private mercury vials
Which they somehow use to speak to each other
On every glassine block
Mirrored line climbing and drooping
Based on a face or anus's whim
Or at least its environment, which is beyond
Intention, I must truly choose to remember this
I was walking to work with him in mind
When standing there in three dimensions
Before me I saw Margaret on a ledge
She often smokes there certain mornings
Projecting brick's serial genius
As the day reflected off her thought
Flung up the scene, and I its actor

Approached that building
As if playing a star snapped in half
And spoke the corresponding lines, her own
Which she accepted with medieval grace
"I ate three things: one of them was swan
Another lily blossoms, but the rest
Was the event itself, which I bled
From its eyes after shaking until decibels
Poured from its spine like a Polaroid
And that has made all the difference"
At the time I meant all sustained notes are Zeno's
This is especially true of hinges
When the door sang every time a student
Left the lecture on sex as a commons

Later that morning, fated to begin and end
To world a new relation, each surface in that particular door's
Hinge pounded another harder and faster, a high ivory key
Within each contact a million claps, which is
To say a million murders
Before I left Callie asked if I would be writing about sex
And I said "No, hinges"
It was like quickly walking through a meadow
In an opposite direction
The pure integrity of space went taut
And rang, and like that moment I have been wanting
To tell you about my life for some time now
I'm just discovering the comfort of the stones
Among this blank disease

I picked up this book and it seemed my life
It was person after person
Who will be on that coastal shelf
Until someone tilts the lampshade at too steep an angle
And the whole thing flames, bringing our house

Down with it, and in that expression
You may detect
My exact shadow for the first time
Scissored from the temperature
And pouring down the stairs
If the man I had seen earlier that morning
Had been my student, my shape
Would have been his first missed class
And my name his second, a failstream beginning to run

I walked past the white university
Filtered rose through a dawn so dumb the clear
Only ended when it hit buildings
The whole city appeared an attic
With traffic moving through its beams
Tails diluted at noon
To form the parade of objects making time
Retract into a syllable's sheath
I bellowed just such a word through that window
To rev space to an appropriate speed
But mine remained posed in your throne
On a pier
In which hours equal sentences and night a page
I crouch over in a game I use to throw your money away

Up all night whitewash called from the dice
When they rolled
And swallowed the fussing surf
In two ballooned gulps as if a singer blaming
Syncopation for rings erupting from his finger
They landed and said "We are seven"
So we won, it opened other actors up, the way one
Stomped down Bound 2 Boulevard
As if breaking straight into one cell from another
Like when in temple I whispered "Suck it, Columbus"

Into the Torah so it would land
And be heard now in the square
Another clatter slapped the stone and sails
It woke the cops we ran along

"Fuck the police" Eric wrote from his room
The song issued from some student's system on the street
And impressionable as I am
I undid their exoskeletons
Like the ribbons they were
Two monuments of speech slipped out
One looked a crab the other a horse
Concretely screaming
And then suddenly stopped
Their bodies clotted at the surfaces
Back into the badge that slips around them
And repeatedly clatters to the ground
I wanted to tell you all about this
So I opened my phone

You sat in silence on the line's other end
With objects strewn in a ring around you
As incumbent daylight slugged the table, static
Saturn speaking back to gravity
My words rubbed my teeth, a vapor
Waiting to be installed in the day's exchange
I wanted to say "Am I more afraid of arrest
Or its vessel?"
Margaret would have known the answer, Eric the word
And Callie the actual question, but you just held the receiver
Up as you plucked drugs
From the receiver tree
The branches foamed, another nerve ghost
Bleeding free

We am a truly personal failure
We stood together blinking in the kitchen this afternoon
You hacked up a lens and it slid down the drain
Capturing a certain c'est vrai of the lips
Before they left your words
And erasing the image the following instant
But who could forget such a picture
It is glued upon mine eyes at this moment
Medicating a sensation of being "camouflaged
With shittiness," a phrase stolen from my office cube
From James, who chats among us here
Blessedly posted within this megaphone's range
Lice bend and blur under his name
As I throw it against the western wind

How rare it is to truly change
A dramatis personae gathers off the page, pink stones
Stacked on one another
Wall of everyone you've ratted out
Most of whom you don't know
As surface is privacy at miles per hour
Which pierced the man from yesterday
And were I to do it over I would try
To swallow the arrow barreling at him
Before the bowsman's message reached you instead, blood
Flying literally in my face
I think and nothing happens, I'm
Not going to lie, it is
What it is

I put my lips to that word's law
And play the bruise between dominions
The instrument a wall erupts from
So far out it echoes back
And with mine to the lawn tonight

This fear is not the laser animating
You into a symmetry, but Gemini themself
Who doesn't need that bag of garbage
That is each other's sibling's half
But here I are regardless not dancing on my own
I flow to my twinship, locked both in a cell and on
Its other side by people speaking
You turn to one of me and leak onstage
How rare to truly change

I.

TO ARRIVE WITH CARTOON DEVOTIONS

1.

White evening & they move. Among them those
who know you, those who will
& those who may, but for the moment keep
glued to cobble, skew the penchant bucking parade's
foresworn progression. A makeshift harmony whistles through
their arms like a squad,
the first tone of the elbow, the second setting off the weave—
some questions posed for your amusement—
when you stand before the mirror, what animal
do you most often mimic; does your mouth
fog out as you step closer; what image bends
between your lips; does it obey the axis given;
what song comes on the radio.
The hundreds lift their arms & raise one finger.

2.

As one element (you say leaves) here unhooks
from what it followed, rightly so, a kind of grace
lights off from where it waited, or was tethered,
if you must, if you allow
that sail will not name wind, as if
a cloud and arc of rain would slip another pitch toward blue
if your umbrella tapped
a moth, the sun, a slice of headlight, falling leaves.

Is this the voice of posing or regard?
You walk the rows with a throat of reeds. What figure
hears your thin resolve; there are those
who catch that redshift nod without police & bells.

"SUCKING THE SHERBETS, CROONING THE TUNES,"

What rooms have listened to your pulse, much less words since the last
time you learned a name? To prefigure
what those ears have diagrammed from memory would be
its own reward this afternoon. There's a kind of duplication of breath
that is architecture in and

of itself, and I think it happens less priestly in statues
than it does in animals, to speak in a voice
composed of empty wasp-nests would also be

its own reward, but you are general and I promised
I would not change the subject. Still, that's just another brocade
in a bedsheet of fleeting votives, like your name's aftermath
when filtered through regional accents, even mine, or the simple
act of lying. It is alarming to be so barefacedly

unvarious by comparison, like waking up to find yourself
transformed into a collection of jars brimming with the same
old white man's piss: as now, to a boy with a forehead like a movie

screen staring at me in the café I'm writing to you in, now he's
opening his mouth, now his beaver imitation
is miraculous, and the water glasses are so clean here
that I cannot help gliding my finger along their rims until an amen
discloses itself as slowly as light dumps from the ceiling.

LIKE A FIRE THE CRICKETS GO ALL MAFIA INSIDE OF

Downstairs the color of music is money. I make no promise
And one is to repeat myself. The album skips
On a track with horns. When you flip the light switch insects
Crouch in the sink, little anthem
Flickering through the pipes. I would like to be arrested with you,

Detention for the duration of a cartoon
Suits. I would hardly accuse you of being an anthem.
When your tendons refuse to be plucked
In a theater of headlights a slack-jawed idiot hangs puppets in my pupils
Like the clowns you scratch out on your lottery

Tickets with a coin. The color of money hidden in them is music.
I rarely return from jail to my door. I watch
Chords of traffic under dun noon,
Try to speak and traffic streams
From the song you are already humming through

Band-Aids covering each of our mouths. Never one
To shirk from my voice when we pass
The lower branches you
Reach and collect a crop of their tickets, place them in my hand.
I count them in the dark, approaching the next in a series

Of streetlights where we are bound to be identified as thieves.
Outside the money of music is color.
I release my promise on a constellation, audible as a band
Of cartoon instruments. I taste my mouth
In reverb's purse, yours walking from my home.

IDLE VEINS CONDUCTED IN GARDENS OF THE IDIOT BOY

Now I hear shit in the grass, one minute
    Glides by on my cells
And two and three as bluejay nests seize up
    The park like thatched wet
Gobs of sleep along some soma's clownish
    Rim. Some tweets meanwhile
Drill white gems to the hymn of several skies.
    The Internet is

Succulent with flies, and so I ribbon
    Earth with honeyed traps
That she might also sleep to strumming wings,
    The little badger.
A toss of plastic pearls swing from a girl's
    Ears like balls, thwhuck thwhick
Thwhuck, air's thick stomach chockablock with bells.
    Some kids slumber in

The asphodels, and as I hear them with
    A light, the humble
Bees drop pollen on their pink-slapped faces
    Then flock into the
Pixilated screen of hives their empire longs
    To sing them back to
To spill through hexagons of hurt. Worms write
    Documents in dirt.

CATS

Let me ruin it for you in saying
When bolts snap on your spine's taser

Poetry pools in the outer, more angelic plume,
Material numeral's fluid firewall.

A gust juliennes my cats
Leaving two fur chandeliers

Lit by future movements, sun's installed
And socket-shaken glare

Beating from bone's mirror as thought
Enters and exits its dock.

Their fresh event now whirs to that limit
Around the room, twin atlas volumes

Read like flip books whose vile jelly
Windows into paper guts—

We see through them but they're still there, I'm
Sure as frost fakes your words

In other of Earth's clawed curtains.
At what hour should we call it night?

Pointing north and south, a reassembled freedom,
Poetry's architectural history grows

Fungal on the number one. I'd love to go
Down facing stars, such mud.

The gathering environment told my
Contagion that these were friends.

PARADISE

It's snowing on the demented
Lions denting
This museum's entrance.
To call it
A library would
Swerve space like
A claustrophobe pissing down his spine
To open his nerve.
Steal yourself.
This the city's
Biggest garbage
Pail fire is our purest future,
Vision in
Direct contact with its line and curve,
Oxygen escaping objects with its
Moxie intact
Because the noun itself's blue
So more equal to its fuel.
You can hear a chopper chomping
At gravity's knob
Somewhere overhead
In approach, mumbling
ODE LOAD MODE ODE
In perfect time
But in this dream there are
No people pressed
Between its pages.
Only one thing's always
Itself a weapon, so
You see when you clatter its cage.

IN THE THIRD PERSON

Evening empties a harbor
As smoke billows into a bedroom
Inhaling the fool in the air
People rush through its channel

As smoke billows into a bedroom
Papers and tablets drowned
People rush through its channel
Resting like questions on a reef

Papers and tablets drowned
But in asking what do I evade
Resting like questions on a reef
In space, invader-lit

But in asking what do I evade
I have little but presence of mind
In space, invader-lit
To give and the mind are a terrible thing

I have little but presence of mind
To give, property snow falls around
To give and the mind are a terrible thing
Your face a circular sting

To give, property snow falls around
I was sore in a number of senses
Your face a circular sting
Absent as a window's weight

I was sore in a number of senses
Cruel as moss blanketing my lips
Absent as a window's weight
Passengers slip out of

Cruel as moss blanketing my lips
Whispering to one another in cuffs
Passengers slip out of
No more or less sadistic

Whispering to one another in cuffs
A guard brutally splayed
No more or less sadistic
Over an exit, and deeply dreaming

A guard brutally splayed
Was raining and it was going to stream
Over an exit, and deeply dreaming
That word I had before, cruel crystal

Was raining and it was going to stream
I seem to have forgotten
That word I had before, cruel crystal
The chemical property's name

I seem to have forgotten
But remember more than I admit
The chemical property's name
And am equal to its melting

But remember more than I admit
Our laughter spilling under the door
And am equal to its melting
From where we once collected

Our laughter spilling under the door
Evening empties a harbor
From where we once collected
Inhaling the fool in the air

A NORTHIST

At least odd numbers feel a square
Banning the riptide, the body in cones,
I like to be ripped back in this certain way.
We crossed through banks, limbs literally light,

Black bills clogged with minnows, so
Disappointed we crossed
Rock-solid oxygen
Into someone's wet refrain. Hurt, I keep my eyes

Fixed to the blank page of her walking
Away and it continues, she drags a special horse
Across the lawn, is years old,
Blank boats pass in the sound and you ask

What I'm reading? If only.
To wear your touch as a suit
Too warm for this room. These battles,
I didn't deign shit astronomical just

To feel waves carve
A room in space between our heads
Because the room is "designs." A sexual arc
In geologic terms, all the moves we learn

Flock to the word they die inside
Having never passed beyond the yard other
Than to throw a boomerang I haven't the heart
To tell them will never return.

And if one ever did? It would mean no demand
For more of us weeping anew as movement. Twitching fins
Dive away from our bodies
On the cusp of us detecting the larger shape attached

And we mourn that experience, text each other
Elegies in swells as it rises with friends
To surface in full noon blinking its jewel like a pearl
And slurps our ribs until they splinter.

You look so bad I don't respond, but with joy
And genuine regard
For our actions, self-appointed
Historians going through grace

Periods until the series punctures the cypress,
Mutes my home.
I like to be assigned to bliss as much
As the first of us though always later

Like when she said, "I would never tell you this
In New York but here
It feels like I'm just talking
To my computer," and as the dock lolled in the next

A cormorant surfaced ten feet off and flew away splashing,
So you're just a location,
Location, location, location, location,
I would say the water inside is better,

And scarlet smears away from this
Vault of pinpoints globed in white corrections,
The commute physical, a glacial kiss
Gathering in legs and arms.

APPETITE TECHNICIAN

My ruler hums on the table's
rim, the wall
a keystroke beating

water through its precinct.
My bee unspools
her throat, for coughing

wings from plastic heralds
sleet. & December
sings its kitchen

in the lamp. I draw triangles
& touch my corners.
Something is against the law.

THE GRAVE OF HIERONYMUS HALFPENNY

Read the sun and one ceases
To be an impossible logarithm
Its sound throws a book of fables
That cuts me just above the eye

In a tomb decorated
For the god of handwriting
A grid in which I never say

The same word twice but infiltrate
A traffic's thrum just as
Your face blurts through the pillow.
Gold is a word

Issuing from the mouth
Of a video game, warm and legible
By night come morning

Brushing a margin's teeth. I
Tie holograms to rafters
So when the thread
Waves the draft's

Source can be detected
As when Puritans
Made branches screech with frost.

It is early in the century
Light bulbs linger
From the nuclear age but
Glass coils replace them night

By night. I have not
Learned to love police
But deeply do the law

For its wattage may be used
To find the force's
Aerial doppelgänger.
A current runs below the trees

A radio wave stalks it, lighting off
The limbs, dark bird reading
Lists of Latin names as if

It were the news
And though those nouns escape
Me as you sharpen
I have faith they will return.

When snow does fall
One becomes an extension of its
Synapse, pink fiberglass and chimney

Yielding a legacy of fumes
Holding the sky in a graph of hours
Rigid with points
Made to order, meadow in which

a) Mail sprouts folded from the trees plus
b) The penmanship with which
They are addressed distinguishes

The hand that wrote them from
A sweepstakes but
c) Contains a history, is one day
Bolting itself to shadow

Requiring a hired agent that
d) Flutters in its wrapping paper
Like the winged insect.

Sun remains the nail
It flies to, hammering on mirror
Neurons, reel of children
Running through me. Children are

Exceptionally cruel but you know
What else is money? Mercury.
Flesh to flesh we

Are string tied to digits air
Uses to run its calculator
Before it pays its taxes
Which judging by my neck's crick

Means today's my birthday.
I age quickly as rainwater ruins
A piano over the earth, the keys

Tighten all architecture
Between two poles, their friendship with
The dead is famous. Songs
Escape me every April and the press

Takes note, they bear six sides
And watch in silence as ferns
Breach my skull, and when

I tag my tears ASTRONOMY
Mark it on an abacus to prove
Come January
We are the coast of technology.

II.

POOR JAMES

Dragging its rose wagon into the channel,
my fossils floated past
the overhead century
on their abdomen raft
which coaxed some sympathetic air from my ear
as I followed its darkening meter; my mother
arrived on the gravel drive a day ago
and under its influence
I coolly heard her crushing stones
above the breeze, and I was no.

     So I was gripped in gravity's mood
above the blooming magnesium
       grove, and when my face
brushed goldenrod
       six feet hence the earth the rash
it gave my iris felt
       but wasn't good.

A sub-malady I heard
was a sad tribe in a happy world
who believe their bones are glass ... perhaps
the eponymous horseman of good Christian's book
was erased from its prelude
when William feared his knee would melt
under the climate of that crystalline jaw.

Am I not too shattered
to say what he saw.
A friend is speaking from sleep's third rail.
His mouth is bandaged in sunlight and holds an envelope of bail,

and touching my mail,
"He hangs from a thunder
but is distinct from its clap."
These words are my thoughts. I think what I see.

So a self is a failure
not of tempo but melody. Thus
I plummeted through plants in iambs,
and when in haste I struck
some surface found it
like an atmosphere rapped about
the ears, not so fabulously rude.

My notes tumbled out on impact
in a design, erupted in
mute font,
            and a slobbish fugue-timed fuck
blew around, circled once more
and declined.

Its message had a fluid edge.
            "I would chop this heat
down to its seed."
            From these decibels I built
a bridge of blurred stone
            from which I now watch
downed branches
            plow around its infant legs.

I thought I heard it most clearly
from behind, but when I intersected with its lyrics
felt this wasn't so.
That was all the labor
I ever learned upon this planet, and in my deeds
and every step I took from it, it showed.

THE CONSTANT PHRENOLOGY

The floor is a ceaseless dream, god of form,
Even chest-deep in a piano of snow I heard it play
The harbor like a board game, as if a scene
Suspends you in its breeze as you travel
A hypotenuse from one order to the next to advance
No figurine. The sea is like
Nights, a wall of chimed triangles

Rippling through flat air. I am the floor.
From that democratic vantage perfume's
Nothing but landscape, an empty room
Issuing the poet populating it as a blip in the vapor
Vacuuming dells and coasts inside its point
To flood the skull and perform a functional
Damage to its liquid crystal

In episodes on strike; in one dream a young cousin
Shows me a picture of a child sitting next
To a ripped bear with button eyes,
White fluff bursting from its limbs. She says
Do you think Lucy is one girl or two? When I wake
I have to write this down before I forget it, first light
Snatches gears out the mechanism, proving

Come morning despite glare's even sheet
Eschatology's personal coming off the mind.
Something out there wants our pain
Filled with this translucent green nectar
That automatically seeps from the eyes
Without our technical effort; my lung is in my skull,
It is poems by the first known human, Lucy.

Is the fourth a boy, the bedside lamp?
The fifth the *Grave of Light* roaring in my error?
A set scene, that book was sitting
On the nightstand bearing a hinge like a citrus,
Hemlock near the window
Had dissolved, replaced by a curtain. All I have
To do is open my eyes and an archived

Feeling arrives, opens its door for commuters
To breathe the real-time aspirin of color.
I remember lines of a poem on law
But also sweeping snow from my hair
In an empty warehouse, though the workers had
Only just gone home. It looked
Like they'd been breaking paper, scraps mobbed

Through the room in the breeze and larger sheets
Glided laterally while confetti flickered
Into piles of pulp on the floor. It
Was good, the forecast had called this getting
More. A security light was on to cut the roving blue
Flooding the bridges again, more proof
The most feeling monolith is a strobe.

FONT

The firewood is whistling but what about one of these iconic
Trees? Sunday
Clung to the pools

On the mountain. Everything on
The outer banks had a thriving sideline & you have to understand
You don't understand

Per se what is happening when it hisses.
A clatter of dishes rises between voices & an online video of rat-tat-tat.
Last night read "Childe

Rowland to the Dark Tower Came" & did not once
Think of atoms. Breakfast
Ensues in regal

Kisses, a laugh like a windmill breaks between the turbine
& titmice clamor to replace
Grammar. My

Teeth need cleaning. So do my teeth.
Vehicles reel through the gills. One's instincts evolve this is
No diary.

DIARY

1.

GOTARO did not move with-
out, he talked over
duck silence, a rental
sulk. The stove could
hurt but Gotaro was blurting
faith in an
algae he made with his
breathing. Here was the
valve, it poured forth a veil.
No one confused
ruination with sails so
Gotaro lit into the limb
of a window. Off in the city
a building breathed

2.

THE LODESTAR cracked and
continued, it purchased
a juice. Herbs grew here
and here as if radio-
active. Gotaro's love moved
with her sleeping and
dreamed of a lobster
replacing her "fever."
Gotaro dreamed a dark
whirl underwater as if
drains emanated no faith
in the lunar; by her extension
his aunt had
gone dog. Truth
boxed in, bounced and
filled the spring

3.

It did not enjoy. Blood
flowed as if Florida. Gotaro
had only been once when he
smoked rock in a plastic
castle and perhaps for
the first time invented size.
It relayed into the
red of intention. He still
at this point had never heard
knives. Secreting one's
voice is not a topical action.
He watched someone's
tiara hum like a lion,
her teeth way beyond epistem-
ological. Vegetables flecked
the coast and Gotaro continued
its contract

4.

GOTARO would be surprised
by the weeping, but then
it was weeping that
invented him. He who
moves with a hazard
attached rests his eyelids
in concrete fog. Did the
neighborhood awaken
like a puppy's face with every
intention Gotaro replaced?
I am not at liberty not
to say yes, but Gotaro's
xylum is a fountain of no,
and when the grass seems least
tactful of objects he points to an iris,
bends down and picks it

5.

GOTARO, committed to an
asylum of song, had great
faith in arrows. Nothing
else understood his
corrections. A funeral is
a fuse box in this book's
basement. No one could
leaf through the sun
and not feel welcome with
the punks underground,
but this is the nature of
reading without full know-
ledge of lockets. Gotaro's
contains his father's face. He
wears it around his neck
and all day, and sounds flow
through the loop

6.

A PIANO equals necrosis,
you can never bring it
anywhere in space but down. The
wind whistles through its
organs, hums. Gotaro is
composing a piece that
hates his hate, chastens
him sharper than sails
slit a harbor. He once
took a harpoon between
his teeth and dove under
houseboats to see what
was living under his
instrument. He found a great
deal with his hands, and
it was soft and speaking

7.

FORWARD WHAT, nimble ligament?
No one knows what you're not
saying, this is the seventh
hour of iteration and
no one's yet busted out
diamonds or praying.
My movements dark and
plenty. The clock strikes,
time for Gotaro to
position his skin in relation
to his friends the stones
and rabbits—their narrows
pulsing out like boomerangs
on the poor, informed—
but Gotaro can always
make other friends. He
bends in the direction

8.

GOTARO is a kind of second-
century friend, riveted
less by the electronics than the
electronics. Steep censure,
was the surface an intro-
duction to day's satellite?
I marked an orbit as it
vacated my pockets, little
ruses someone else
delights in when the
point from a to b
proves discursive as a
bolt. Gotaro plays from
here to there, his fur
pricked on the back of some
else's neck. It moved,
I found it moving

9.

THE CACTI crumbles between
our tongues, fleet blood
about to get extremely observed.
He shades his eyes and
takes a slug of mirage,
it conceptually cools
him. Perhaps he was
wrong to think a body
could reach him. All he
ever wanted was to
sail across land as if
belief were cut from
each pore as a choice. What
he didn't realize was
faith isn't a spigot, it's a noise

10.

THUS I AM inwardly my police.
I know not where a fly
goes in its pride. Dream in
which a medium friend
drives past me waving in a
roundabout cracks open, not even
enough to jam one's foot into
the other room. Gotaro's is always
in the door, indeed his
feet are not so much
inside them as around.
He walks on his own
two surfaces and
directs traffic in his sleep,
screaming 美は真実,
真実の美しさです at SUVs

11.

GOTARO would rather chill
his face against the frozen
concrete for the rest of
the afternoon than go back
to work but he realizes
too that frost is its own labor,
and unlike the one Gotaro
does for a living this
crystal licking the outer
edges of his frame
is an incision. The
whistle blows, black notes
pour forth. Gotaro peels
himself off the ground
in gradations. He will remember
each as a color on
the flip side of a cut

12.

SOMEONE'S KNOCKING on this
skin like it's an institution.
Draft trickling through his
passageways to meet white
cells. I await your imitation.
Blasted on neon spleen,
felt the opulence implied
in patching up my finest shirt
sewn to another emper-
or. In this sense the needle
frees the present tense
of both legs, lion
gnaws on one like bubble gum
and punctures day's doorknob.
The brass bleeds

III.

ANTIBODY

Judy's window twinkles with primer
I sleep in headgear tailored for saints
Films about animals shine on the ceiling
A crab beams through our hair
The meadowlands are fragile with stealing
They wave their blades in green complaint
Day is a doorbell fucked with error
We have grown tight in the sun
Rivers fatten with animation
And light repairs to a thicket of guns
They do the police with genuine feeling
A factory gathers behind the rain
I salute the logical weather
Judy's window twinkles with paint

PAPYRUS FAIL

The body inflates a small revolt
As it rests for its return.
Sound carries well in damp weather, as do ferns through skin,

And a wood is a print-out of its history with space
Provided for mutation
Which the poet tells us flowers and people

Are almost never favorable to the organism
At hand. I wonder if swans count.
To bear the stain of involvement

Relentlessly as a jigsaw puzzle; I don't want
You to see me see you be fire.
All of my actions are toys at the podium, even

When sailors strike. A diamonds king,
That's a good example of what it feels
Like to die inside those numbers. One slits

The end of autumn open and what does she find?
One, and that has some bearing on us meeting here
Tonight when the alphabet's twilight bangs

On a classical procedure toward weeping.
Let me demonstrate by reading
A few scenes out of my face: metal and Elizabeth have many

Children, but metal meets a man
Inside years. How could this happen?
Well for one, what got into it was sleep,

Blocks of, shocks blown
Out of the belt moving seconds
Through the factory exploding hours into others.

Thriftless units,
Let them remain for the tête-à-tête.
For another, I'm filing them to a sharp point as we speak

But the inspection is already over. It concludes there is a hole,
Income leaking patients, and the flow's
Not cold if you spread them into your hands and rub friction

Until it loves you in return. This is an irresponsible poem
Because I think I can reasonably assume
Even filled with a fluid

You would not activate it under the present dome.
One cannot simply call
A ghost on the telephone. Lead poet, what was it

You had meant to plagiarize off breath
When you opened the furnace
And slipped this little letter inside? Who else would have read?

The police are increasingly after my friends, but
What about the nouns departing? Where's one to plant
These lost puppets? I fall

Asleep each night with little faith you want to reveal,
And that particular ember of lack
Does not contain enough fuel to heat even this small room.

Nothing goads its borders, so what good could red do now
Unless suffused with what I hope and imagine
Might be your tactile alarm?

It's not often you get to really feel dominions clapping
But what you feel right now
Is the back of your own neck, not mine,

And at least this month both of us are living therein.
While we're here, do you think you could lend
Me the brisk hammer that an heirloom

Is?
Now nails, now gentle force, now photos hung
On walls. In the future

Thought will be extracted from our eyes like a roll of film, negative
Spilling its shrill sequence
In braids to ape the state's

Novel way of chastising any speech remaining
By recording it with the exact same voice
And then dubbing

Cartoon eyes over its decibels,
A plausible direction for where we might go next imagining the soul
Via arms. It's not punishment, just

How maps drink a system. Remember how you once
Kissed a map
And it was cool and bottomless? I sometimes forget men and women

Even have legs but something
Operatic out there
Reminds. It enters

When I'm not that far in the grieving
Largely because each cube of air
Ends with a cube of its larger organization; try

As you might we do not have the vocabulary to glow the way
Away from me, but I hope you believe me
When I say I mean harm. Truth's threat

Is several friends raking laughter up
To store it in black plastic bags, burning it with poison ivy,
Then picking up the phone only to breathe all

Over the dial tone. So many calls
I keep forgetting to insert letters (in the traditional sense of the word)
Like lava, a son in the flickering sea,

Forgets to knock on the water's surface
Before it says hello to a temperature. Something smells fishy
Here but only to the eye. I know you less

In collaboration, like a mower
Blocking day as fast as day trembles
By any other name. Inside

A disastrous future awaits
Though beautiful in its process. Of courage
All I know to say is

Night is longer than the heart
In certain of its variations, namely
The one beaming between.

Of course water is an emotional experience, you wouldn't
Want to run through it protected.
I've known those people

And they were all landscapes
Versus your shape, they have a kind of session in aspens
As a smattering of aspens

Shares a single root system, the mountains in a view
Revolve around one blazing core so hilarious with goo
That to call it metallic is I mean excuse me?

No one wants to eat
Off of that thing with a collection of glands
To make holy each day. The river says "huh," and I have to disagree,

If not with the inflection
Then the implicit question's size
Looming in its frog-flecked filigree. Last night passed,

The water now green. My first breath this morning an analog
For the eye's
Entanglement with transparency—so the river's not

Shrugging, it's beginning to say "Hamlet,"
Muffled in the opening rain. There's danger in inflection.
Father of emblems

Lead me to some stuff by the river
If you flash on the surface in several shades, if you are
Or live in its surface and small waves.

Five years ago I drove along the other bank
And thought about "orchard" versus "vineyard,"
Now I am older, don't think in words,

And it still gallops
Down the banks like fuck. The poet also
Gives off speed, rate at which we become

Nurses for each. I stand there in the waiting
And finally glide to the fridge
Which is here for a visit and itself

Bright as a hospital. Must be all the fumigants.
The power reminds that plants are not kingmakers,
A politics ought not be wielded

For aesthetic sheen alone,
Fastening flowers to a gun of infinite referents. It's dark in there,
I find my cell while rooting inside, open it and say

Come home, but the receiver is already there.
This is another reason for teeth,
The forehead

Can only chew through so many surge protectors.
Someday I'll proceed
With that action with evidence. I need

To share something at you, and it's what
You do with them: people get Europe pulled
Out of their fingernails, enter a diamond,

And what do we find? I find Elizabeth
And she is saying. They
Find a centipede eating a reader. You find an opinion

Pulsing with silence there where light throws hate at a rainbow
But the question remains
Did it heal you with sound?

Because solitude is green and unavailing
And speech is a station through which round weeds blow.
Even I am approaching your throat.

NEST EDIT

You'll wake up in a house with: Green and pink
Furniture: Bowl-shaped ceilings: Water served in plastic:

Lampshades aged variously: Rooms silent like
Plastic: Bowl-shaped and constant: A screen tilting variously

At voluble angles: Your friends will be sleeping: The curtains
Drawn variously: Your friends all in advertising: Serving furniture ·

To friends: Waking up tinted: To paused green curtains:
A history of plastic: Pink to detection: As plastic does:

To yellowing photographs: To your couches and
Lampshades: To water when screened: By your various friends

WHITES

In the clear
    Dust is skin in reverse,
    Its interstices ironed by
        The snow so far as it's received, falls
Like my handwriting was parallel
        Lines, a six-sided
        Die. Searchlights scraped the sea and

We overheard swells,
    Dr. Williams said to the stingray
    No ideas but in thinging
        And the wind died up
More mythic. Vertebrate flag
        Launching to block
    An atmosphere we're doomed to wear

As helmet, we're so fucked even our ruins
    Polish air off
    With towering glass, so when socio-
        Paths stop in the frozen evening
Beyond their wooded minds
        It's for dark deeps
    They think they're not riding. Time

Splashes. Are we evolving fast enough
    To approach one's patience
    Like a train? Here.
        It follows underground just as a tunnel
Ascending open space ceases
    To literally be,
    Exfoliates semantically by dusk, dull gold

Light locking into tresses and
     Aquatic air pummeled by wind
     And and. The mirrored vessel
        Shakes the shipwreck
Off its skin
        To hit the target harbored
    In an iris

Thinking if it's there
    The outdoors must
    Be shield until centuries never
       Were; a flock of chrome doves
Coos like a bruise
       In a ring around the Prison Ship Martyrs
    Monument as I move

Through sun as it falls down my spine, the scene
     Shadow-globed but floodlit 24/7. It says
     Put your money where this lighthouse
       Spikes its under-urn. I am 29.
When will I die? I incline
       Not to the question's spectacle,
    Not that it's too early for

That Orphic pile of media AKA the prodigal son
    To sing, but
    Because no mirror mars me
      Beyond visible core, got to get
Out of this armor, no patent on the apparatus on
     Which we lean is law-
    Compelled to flower

And meet me as my upright
    Torso jogs across the land
    Sheathing "revolutionary" lungs
        As a cypress marks
The turn in a race, so those gas tanks
        Will be my quiver of arrows
    Whose contents fail to spill the village

In a poem but do so on the street,
    I'm looking forward to becoming an environment
    In which day collapses more
        Like chess
But motivation falls from a knight
        Forward and to the side,
    So that hope and action are as much a mystery

To themselves as you, beloved grid.
    Fact is I have too lately
    Realized I'm fatal
        Pinched between our theater and index
Crossing the Manhattan Bridge like a castle
        Equally in costume
    And uniform. Now

We travel together
    Through the open
    Air like a coin into a tomb, like here
        We rain glazed albatross
Depending on much red transportation
        And all we
    Touch turns to plasm, so here

We are beside ourselves.
         Blue lights blast from cars, my dust
         Blowing up, maybe you saw
                  My own tone runs us
To our windows and fails, freezing my hide
                  Under midnight deluxe
         With miles to go at this kingdom's margin

Switching our tail.

RENT

A Quaker graveyard
where suicide hotlines
end in a crumpled bow,
everywhere I live
I see and where I don't
splash blindness in my wake,
hang bells on smells
that prick my skull
with ancient skill.
So when fluorescent
gym lights tangle
down into our bed
from across the alley or
someone shrieks in
public transportation,
it never abrades me
as it always stuns
our interlocutor. Limbs
cut into this space
we pay for conversation.

OUTLET

And passing through my throat a light

Wind off the engine's
Wake   lamps swapped in and out with plans
Some winged ringers for their freight

I have not hurt nor ebbed hurt in the bud

Blunted garden lights its
Seed   blunted worms beam out and fan
A middle finger for green breeze

And sirens husk their ampersands

CHAMPAGNE YEAR

In chrome we were functional
I'm talking metal for our lives while eschewing skeletal gold
Like span and flex and generation, canines all

Sharpened under a land inhaling
Persons as if it had given
Up on rain, but weather's not information it only wears its shirts

And like la migliora fabbra sang this shirt is how I feel.
For you was sunburnt I are leaving we am buoyed by
Homages before day drops hits.

I do not think an occupation
Will teach us how to live but it may well teach us why to
And I welcome that stricture clean-willed as

Entertainments
Pierce sleep's flow in waves of interview
So I am assisted by a radiance of bending

From corpus
Into a paperclip to slip onto a chain
So the breath exchanged in conversation will be a sitcom that not only

Bathes the room in blue light but may be remembered in
Waking, sweeter than the via dolorosa David
Letterman nightly took us on with all his stupid teeth. God knows movies

Turn us toward a castle and me I'm processing being on holiday first with
Then inevitably from votives, so.
Do you follow? On

The twelfth day of the twelfth month of the twelfth year of
The twenty-first century let's
You and I meet from a variety of angles like magnets with a history

Rotating titanium flame, then pry each other
From its fingers
Strictly for the feeling of extracting other nouns from emitted light

Into a reflected one
Perforated with verbs as plentiful as rocking horses and wooden swords
Our tongues once made iron, for with our tongues

Myth flows of its own volition, washing
Machine packed with bedsheets worn as capes. Perhaps the sheets are
Waves they are waves. Between us flows a school

The tint hid you. Something about being in hell, and having no duties because of it. That tilt into freedom. I've never been so, eject my previous works, break with them like a vine entering an Egyptian organization of stone fallen into common apex obsolescence. Its walls come out in fistfuls and the dead flower through. To walk through the plaza with a biological diagnosis folded in your back pocket, the evening folded ahead of you. I felt the full radius of your sobriety when you said this "sounds adult." The people walking by were wet with conversation. In a damp room dense with fellowship the laser point slides up my corpulent surface and my back leg lives alone in a room whose rent is no dollars.

Nothing is this easy. The move is sociopathic, it demands and then rejects more than is possible in a given life—you just crane your spine and move its maximum volume. A dimensional eroticism, like kill everything that's dead in me. I have this tender hatred for all we nearly are. Airplane shadows slide over the meadow protected from hollow heaven, laughing as the streetlamps flash their balls in the breeze. A class of children spill around them and run out all the exits at once. I open my eyes and recognize more faces than I thought the mind allowed in its "yellow pages," I see the coats of arms from friendships past crystallize at every glance: in the train, on the street, the news, at my job and other job. My own face drops like a glove in the shade. Baby spiders pour inside. Drums drift through the trees. The golden hour. I come to my senses at an awful party, bodies twitching all around us, dipping their mouths to the libertine hole in the air, the East River framed by the wall-sized picture window behind us glittering evil in cinemascope nightfall. A poet turns to me and says, "You've totally exceeded my expectations of you."

And what were we seceding from? The weather was too wrong for running. An ambulance echoes more in rain, water being more reflective than what it protects. This is its signature style—style defined here as everything exceeding function. And in that sense a truly emergent tool; there are ring tones that run abreast with music rising from the pit but always one tying tripwire between the hedges. Plucked, it rings a perfect C, and the emergency passes into my legs. As I find you only get to spend what time it isn't. It isn't 12:34 in the afternoon, a shadow past the solstice in 2015. We three travelers reddening around a single sunset. A badness mothered under Advilean amber dripping from municipal sycamores whose limbs line the edge of this cirrus ceiling. My God it is adhesive. And who was the tron that walked beside you peeling its song from the floor?

IV.

COLLECTED ANTHEM

Lay your stutter in the creek.
Fuck the the around the moon.

SNEAKY FUME

For several weeks I have preferred to enter a room
Dripping with news
Transmitted from a fleet of wooden tongues, their lips
Flickering under the thicket of fists they feint
To aspire to in front of their children.
Children prefer to wear gloves in the summer.
I prefer to enter a room of news.
It has motivated me closer

To hobbies I have long wanted in my range. The mandolin, no longer
A wig upon my bureau, climbs
My skull and sings from the bald, bright as the cockatoo
I will obtain
As soon as I have learned the finger
Work required to play "Auld Lang

Syne" without my fingers, given how cold
My house will be by then. She will give the impression of playing it
Without me. My hobbies are contagious.
Thus the mailman's paroxysmal doll collection. He is too aged
But then so are children. So are their dolls.
A news of dolls arrested me yesterday on my
Lawn as if I had inhaled a gulp of the pool

That their eyelids are now manufactured with plastic. Mine remain
Swollen as lifeboats

From prolonged exposure to sun and chlorine. It is agreeable to share
A cigarette with the mailman to keep
Oneself apprised, one fist
Stuffed with kindling and the other with news. For a duration

We speak to each other and then I stamp it out when it burns down
To the filter, my foot
Licking the grass with its ashes before

Retiring inside to the copse of rooms where
My model transportation lies. I am arguably a genius of trains and
Boats so long as they are tiny.
Children grab for them from my windows until they
Learn to otherwise prefer what might
Happen to their hands

When I catch them in the act. Parents muddle my doorway in
Zodiacs of fuss, as if the tears littering my windows were
Sugar sprinkled in my engine, invented theater
In which their sons and daughters pen
An accord I trollishly burn in the wings while I broadcast letters on
The sly crowing what joy I
Harvest from their woe, gaudily immune
To the alarming silence creeping into our friendship.

BONE MACHINE

Fathom this countdown

What if to say   It is radiant ugly

That'd be your anthem

Beautiful as boots becoming belonged to by knees

.

Slug trail   owl wing   deer shit &
Fern   Fuck

The police?   you sang to the evening

They are dust to the light bulbs
We see by in cities

The pollution not   of music, but horses

INDEPENDENCE DAY MANIFESTO

I found my finger glued to my front door.

I walked inside and a music stung me with its index.

And in the absence of finger my fist punched my piano.

And in the absence of finger my smile withered orchards.

And in the absence of finger my orchards canceled.

And in the absence of finger my orchards chewed mirror.

And my mirror loosened.

And my rivulet ran like stone.

And my stone was money.

And my money was a hole.

And my hole was running money.

I bought a hive of friends to teach me how to speak.

And in the absence of bees my mouth ran dry.

And in the absence of tongue.

And my moon bit through its bag.

And my bag wept constellations.

And my constellations rusted.

And my rust purchased stamps.

And my mail flowed.

And I found that finger posted, speaking its math.

I found my finger speaking to fingers, a silent number of.

POEM ENDING WITH THE SOUND OF CROOKS

Passed through that afternoon's
Slot, we were waving
Our names in its face, poised to gun

Our own fair faces down, sun clicking
Coins, that tenure ended fast as blue falls
Into black, and with

That famed threat's fleeting
I froze rooked of dark
And paid and

Froze again, exited and drew the well
A pail of white creatures,
From night work they turned

My wrist convex with united
Kicking, which in its grace
Blunted our own faces'

Grace in return, we were not heads
Packed with eyes but
Eyes with teeth

Chewing the blue out of day
And swallowing ad
Infinitum, I froze

And dialed but you refused my calls, still
Fast in your fist a crumpled
Slug, even if the torque

Was fake the sound was realer unloading
Our names from its shell.

FROM THE SIGNAL TOWERS

The perch appearing   hammered through

to flint a wing from gray to gray
to hum the vowel that earns a name

.

I'd like to tech
my voice to seaming

dusk to blue
                attrition's speed

If I told you the branch was like not
nail, but screw

would doves   still fall   all into line

I'd like to be abreast of every word assigned

For every hammer   a fist of pins
a bolt to be   a bolt abiding

SNEAKY FREEZE

Wolfing the temperature my tongue fuses
Shut the pin affixing each white page
To its filth's blue ribbon, the snow outside a microphone
Flaring my little throat

Out six years longer than one word announces the counter-clockwise
Ticks untangling canaries from
The net of hands they sleep in. Hard to love them, little birds,

Dumbly buying every seed I sell.
They don't even know my name. For one my name's
Shitty, for two I have neglected sun
For the tenth time for

Shitty weather, third my friend is coughing
Ruggedly in the room I left her
Sleeping in without a lozenge, fourth she is not sleeping, so

I have lied again, a game you doubtlessly
Know by heart by now, for hard to love them as it is it's
Harder to swallow them, even washed down with a glass of snow,
Harder still to vacate to sleep before finding the pencil I need for

Sketching other animals
With when planning to build them out of weather, the latter a rolling
Action you also need to master, but that is neither

Here nor there yet. For building one with teeth
First instead of wings enter the first one's teeth
Into your book stained
Glass, a mouth to live in with light available only

In the six hours surrounding noon, the working ones,
So in fact not hard to love so
Much as the thicket from which this error

Clips its thorn's a destination, office
Vacant of petals and waiting room magazineless, no game
In which the gifts dispersing alarm in music are even mine
To sell. I sell doors,

Insist plants not be heard through the dripping January's
Wolves give off. If fixed to the appropriate season melt them
Twice for what's bloomed in their stomachs, but today I fold

Lying still, plucked
From the bleachers you are accustomed to seeing perched on by a shadow,
Eyes stapled to the stage in grass's
Stadium waiting for clean feedback, for the grass deleted

Here's nothing but a lip for its field and less than two-thirds of my
Bed is occupied by an audience, decade spent in bed
Talking trash to my alphabets and eating them illuminated.

A RUBBER LION

The future resided
In everything, waves cooling
My surface come morning,
And wrecked it never

Circles back, though
This is its flowering action,
Rising again with debris.
Poetry is like the end.

We cut us open and
Said the knives
Were too pretend, the atmosphere
Our second skull.

It opens a like a novel.
Kissing couples in the park
Recede into the tide
And my cats swipe at the anima-

Tronic pigeons dropping
Statuary from behind
The wave's window; rain in this city
A glass kind of statue. And all

The little creatures vibrate
Over the problem geode
In this pornographic daylight.
I realized this year that that

Was also a source, the angle
Predators strike from,
A fish from below—
The scholar stabs

It like a dictionary, then stabs
It like a person.
What law is at work
Ensuring my own organs remain

Invisible to the Sunday market?
Sprinting through food,
Swimming to an avuncular country
To end up in a foreign square,

Memorials common as acid rain,
The aftermath of Katrina
Is what one might not call
"Nice in the shadow"

As pausing in summer
To drink from a cool vessel
While riding a pantoum-like bull.
I inhale its breath

And a full-blown neurology
Enters my cave, a charge
Circles the ladyslippers.
I step outside to greet it

And a fleet of sand goes aero-
Dynamic under my feet,
Everything I have I leave
To this amnesiac plot

Soaked in its theft, and who's to say
This is what the personal demands?
Thus paying the electric bill
In an open box of wind—

Cats of the ancient Internet,
You might say I "always already"
Feel them among us here and there,
The Chaplinesque endorphins

Entering the camera like
Lines with their chests
Removed but revived—
CRESCENT SUN and A RUBBER LION

Scroll across the flat
White bombadier as it films
All four walls of this
Crysanthemum swagger glass

In which an Orphic anal plug
Regards your surface.
But this is lost on us: no
Staring into bridal time

For those marking its burn
Across my brow as your footfall
Crosses the ceiling,
A cop dropping pollen,

It's redundant to fear
Technology in a poem, as one
Or the other is like the end.
Thus the real cats crying

As they sense—what else
Do they do in this cramped
Apartment?—the net I speak is
Bankrupt of wind, and when

They can't adorably murder
All earthly dignity
They know plus one
Crashes on the shore.

V.

DRAMATIS PERSONAE

Luminal, my house
smells like a forest of piss. It seems mountain
bedrooms have been wandered from
the singular topography of & pine

is making preparations for a second
private dialogue with hush. Is it
possible I deserve exactly
your intentions? I have heard a chant for, for example,
grass for sea for song for flesh,

rasping on a kind of stone in cadences
mistakable for nothing but
the work of the blade, its voices sunning
too early in the afternoon
to expect benign rendition, &

I was afraid. Remember wearing that sling
last time around? One-degree history
of snip, what bones
you have leak work on my eyes.

THE POLICE

All three of them are desperate: their great guilt,
Like poison given to work a great time after,
Now 'gins to bite the spirits. I do beseech you
That are of suppler joints, follow them swiftly
And hinder them from what this ecstasy
May now provoke them to.

(Gonzalo, *The Tempest*)

Speech is the fourth wall made permanent & at its window
Prayer collects, modicum of hot noise
Insisting in a fog we find the breeze & greenery beyond the glass
    most critical.
Hours clench their fists & begin
Nursing candlelight modeled after the soliloquy of winces
Vincent Price delivers on horseback, lack of British accent
    brazenly flickering
Witchfinder General (1968), I cannot verify
The features of the sunset on the evening
I watched that movie projected

On an island in a Northern state, July (2011). In
A subsequent dream he & his horse upbraid me when I
Describe the electric
Current running through them to you, I say to Price (of the horse)

Let it eat a hot aglow
White magnesium blend of oats & apps
To animate some running
Not in its feet but spine, & they

(Price, the horse) snatch
Apples from my briefcase faster than anyone moves even in movies. Then
   I wake.
They were correct

To steal, I wasn't even really speaking
To them so much as you in a fuzzed prototype of what turns out
To be this essay,
Presenting myself as a salesman of apples
Rather than a holy ghost
As other apple salesmen will.

Do you see how already in my account those unremembered features
(Of the movie, not dream) are flattening to a billboard
Magnetizing your gaze up from some interstate's white lines
Toward a romping airbrushed puppy & beaming

Child, so that if you are to trust me to not bleed you of your
   brain's money
Today I have to be equally against whatever I'm selling & the light
   it emits?

In the movie Price & the horse drone rough woe
Trotting o'er the land
In a series of sinister nasal eruptions concerning the whipping of witches
Between shots of various actors' wide eyes & buxom screaming.
Outside the ocean flicked
Light at the house, seals burped on their rock behind a fat wad of cedar
   & hanging
Moss. That the horror should be taken as comedy
Watching it transpire on a bedsheet screen

With a collection
Of stoned middle-aged men was reflected in their
Interrupting to briefly bear kitsch's thick shit

For us with a dramatization
Of their own. Vexed, they said things like

It's not the hottest hot
Chocolate I've had but it
Will do, &
What's going on is he hitting
Her this is horrible, &
Rain makes a hooligan
Out of the soundtrack I can't hear the actors

It is now impossible to remove these men from the movie,
It would be like editing out the horse, Price straddling thin air five feet
    off the ground.
They were too high to listen to anything, it was they who were
    masterpieces,
Price watched them from the screen
& dropped his weapons. It
Darkened & those I love slept to the west so I joined them believing

Art stalks us in broad daylight anyway, child with blade
Drawn to slit our throats as we cross through a country
She calls home & stays young in, always forgetting that our throats
    are billions
& our breath spills between.
But forgetting our power is requisite as deliberately confusing the sound
Of a fire truck over the hill
With a wolf's cry. Art needs us no less than we
It. Otherwise the poor kid follows to our cities
To grow old long before spilling
A drop of our blood.
Behind her grown-up villains, born with beards,
Follow all & never die.

Some weeks
Before seeing it you & I walked
Over the Brooklyn Bridge in

Rain without speech, though
That conversation was of a glamour
I did not know I knew how to submerge my brain

In much less physical hands,
For we are only pronouns & as such suffer through deserts of
    dulled nerves.
We walked in a net
So large the district
Slipped through one of its holes, taxis' dry
Groans like houses
Gathering the glow of an evening meal. If it means hosting nightmare
    like stiff wind
Sails I'm not
Sure one needs
To be so quiet, there are other modes of transportation. But
Need squeaks out from holes in demand & demands rust according to
    our speed.

I would be leaving for another hemisphere in the coming
Months & in the interim was taking a crack
At selling you on the benefits of keeping track of our faces &
Voices via Skype
Instead of languishing in their absence for that duration, hoping to allay
Your fears that this program was a load of shit & would garble
The both of us into delayed beeps & pixels, though I was also a bit of
    that mind.
Despite our advances we have not found a clear way to speak over oceans.

One morning in October you woke & told
Me you'd dreamed I'd been campaigning for it, I'd said

You won't hear
My actual voice but a tone
Of it played on saxophone don't
Worry they will still be my actual
Words only spoken
In actual saxophone, & proceeded

To show you a shot of what my face
Would look like on the screen, bone structure & features intact
But with alternate translations of flickering color.
You remained unconvinced but were
Coming around when you woke.

It is not impossible to fit & channel love
Through a glowing two-dimensional
Plastic screen but it sucks.
Something of the flesh thereby transmitted

Did not feel as regal as it should have to the eye alone,
Not for one's features
But the spell they cast, like a metaphor about pheromones
In which literal smells enter the face, one
I am not capacious enough to invent at this juncture
Where I am trying to speak
In a grammar quick with weeping.
Given our circumstances together under this hot blue lid
Love requires better access to somatic swoon
Than poetry can bear.

It must be repeated
Until the figure hardens into something liquid
As the human frame, not impossible
For if you are reading this transmission
Chances are our heartbreaks at this point in history
Are more or less alike than ever.

I have been better about being alone
In recent years but waking
Up next to you had come to feel like having lungs, adamantine &
Hilarious. Moving away in December
I did not want to be reminded silence is vestigial
Or for that matter ever leave you again

So I'll swallow
Whole days shaved off a life in a country I might have known
But never did. I did not know how to tell you about air,
Nor now
Even inside the parcel of this attempt.

When we did speak lo
& behold it was delayed in the wires. You hung
Up on me once in anger
& though I might have deserved & it's adolescent to do so I will admit
It, I wanted to die
As much for knowing
That so many others have felt crippled

Endlessly by something as fleeting
As fighting with a lover
As for the dumb clang

The program's receiver made when
You retreated from that window
& went back to the winterized rooms in the States I felt a cartoon version

Of myself was already living in
An even more inert Pinocchio,
Wan & drawn by Disney.

I took to the streets
Looking to foster attention constellations
That would protect us from the ill we
Foist upon one another unwillingly
Without ever thinking that love, against
Our beliefs & wishes, seems
To require it
In hot multitudes of names & inflections beyond what an hour's exchange
    can bear,

Such invention required & in love invention
Is as difficult a gift to give another as ever,
Wanting neither fire nor water we do our people in police's voices.
But when no one wanted to talk outside I went straight
Back to the screen. I've never seen so many movies.

        •

In November on the way to hear poets read you & I were pulled over
& though I had only been speeding the young officer
Clad in sunglasses despite the clouds & bruised light
Asked me to step out of the car &
Accompany him in his cruiser
While he ran background checks. You shrugged & I,
A little alarmed
By exposure to a force
Coiled more tightly than my own
Followed him & fixed
Myself in his front seat. He asked if this was the first time
I'd seen one of these from the inside

& I said it was.
Behind us, bottled in a clean & perforated plexiglass pane,
A German shepherd continued completely losing her shit.
The officer told her to shut up
& as he ran the program on our licenses he asked what I did.

I told him I was a teacher
Though the truth was I was unemployed.
Ashamed of the lie, I added
I was also a writer. At this he looked up.
He asked what kind of writing I did. I said poetry.
He smiled,

& I don't think I'm lying to think I discerned a muted affection, but will
    never be certain
As sympathy & contempt often run the same drills
On the field of the face.

What kind of poetry.
I told him that was the hardest & worst
Question he could ask, & at that he laughed.
I told him most of it didn't rhyme
& he repeated that out loud.

He asked if I knew any of my poems by heart
& at that I laughed,
Said I didn't, but wanting to offer something for his seemingly earnest
    curiosity revealed
A key poem in the book I was writing was titled
"Appetite Technician." He nodded & thought about that for a moment,
    asked
What's the title of the book?
I never thought to ask his name.

Another dream. Six horses write on a wall, their pencils repeatedly
Clattering to the floor. They coat their hooves with
Rubber cement & step on the pencils with superannuated care,
Continue. Piles of shavings litter the ground around them.

Their riders sit at a nearby table playing
Online poker, but when the wind
Picks up the Internet
Fails. The riders curse & mount the horses,
Ride to a meadow where the connection can be repaired. Given to
    fright when
The offending riders root for their whips,
The six horses run together

From wall to meadow, & when they arrive they pick a variety of pens
    from the
Grass with their teeth.
When the riders are finished gluing wires they remount.
Tired out, the horses trot
Back to the wall with the pens. But
Six more horses have arrived at the site

Without riders, painting
Over the pencil. They turn & stare at the first six with brushes
Hanging from their mouths,
& the riders dismount to inspect the new designs.

A gesture runs deeper than the improbable
Stone, someday the sun will have swatted
Our friends underground where our childhood toys are buried & will
We then wish to share a bed with strangers

& speak with them about all we know who have continued
Against the promise of a grid
Diminishing even as its points sharpen into hyperbolic focus when
    evening settles down?
The reading lamp goes on,
It does a different chemical

Reaction than other light upon the skin
& at that I do not know.
A trust between all inert objects punctures night
Such that we are forced to admit that nouns are either alive or more
Active than we have imagined
& this is also involved
In our capacity to learn not only how to love correctly
But the survival of our species.
As for the former
It seems I can only write this when we are apart, so perhaps as strangers
We might learn to love to critical exhaustion

The versions of each other who remain avatars
For functions impossible to be performed except in a state
Of radical & unknowing patience
Which works more brightly when subsumed into the muscle
Of our waking lives, so it's no mistake we want to fuck
Now as I write this sentence in May, your breath the only grammar
I want to see in color before the night is over,
Your speech & glances made mythic by the fact that it is you who speaks.

But even myth refutes demands
Submitted in the story so far as it's been told,
A wolf wails in the distance & on the mantle above the fireplace
A key spins in a little horse as she slows her hooves
& when she stops the room slips into a capable darkness.

May this invention issue a multitude of orders
& may you disobey them all
That shatter records will shore their action
Against our luminous attention to beam beyond a flat & white refrain.
Plucked from the ground
Like ribbons from a gift box packed with a doll,
Earth needs our bones gliding over it precisely less
Than we the song issuing five or six feet above the green.
The decorations who make the gift thoughtful
Should not be confused with the doll itself in all its mute & painted
     glamour,
As living matter, plastic cells
Lush with the spell
Of carnal affinity flinging through our veins, is not the same as life.
We love the world for what it reflects as much as for what it contains.

Now in July others I love sleep far from the coast &
I have trouble remembering my own dreams, rendering the one
About Price & the horse remarkable for its knife-edged amplitude, even

If you will never know whether or not my actual words were a lie
To move you into believing, as belief is the only house
We are told we are built to sleep inside.

The movie sleeps in the air itself, the men in its glowing reviews.
By the light of that candle it is Price & the horse
Who are a house,
You & I are not until cold wind & rain incorporates
Us into its virus of bedtimes, though on the bridge

We were soaking
Wet & money,
Here I am again continuing to drag you under that roof.

All the sunset does in memory is bloom like a brand, gold pill dissolving
Into the body of water nearest our pillow.

I'm not against the sunset but its problems
In advertisements are myriad as sleep.
I recommend you go outside, see one with your own two eyes &
I'm not selling anything free. Here is another dream for no money.

The window weeps
A bag of light
Into the bedroom, white clatter
Chased by humming filaments

& you place your face still as flint by the light
& your face clicks
& fills with liquid. A holy ghost runs from your eyes
& nose, a holy ghost green on your sleeve
Winds its way down amalgams of streets with you while you speak
    to strangers
& at home even your ice cubes pray in the dark
& the dark weeps, sneezes
& as night drives in its wilted nails Price hacks the coffin an unscreened
    window
& the holy horse freezes.

11 September 2011 − 4 July 2012

GLASS HORSE

1.

The sea can do things that are almost amusing. And to think
it thinks some spells are conductive, and goes on letting
you believe just what it does. Given the salt it isn't
unreasonable, if you deem air
malleable, this present air.
Our fathers are laughing, and the waves.
Allow me to dwell on this. The trick I believe is our fathers

already abundantly there for the bending,
abundant as rocks the sea generates.
It is a matter of selecting

from the menu of temperatures your face is
pressed to even as we speak. A meteorologist
rides a horse out of a forest to find us sitting here by the sea.
His robe drenched with paint, perhaps glue.
He is whistling, he hums
and then gulls flying away, the former melody
gulls pinned to the sky. Are you watching him as

2.

We were trying to build serious
grasses, lamping baseball in its fiction.
Before departure darkened those strings
sunset busted from my lip, but now
it's balding, the field replacing its mouth with graze or the useful
armor blue slips from our house,

from the window, a mammal.
I watched one leave the kitchen and another chase and
the scene immediately misused, a small
motor piece in Technicolor's
dialect gone rogue, an illustration when we

needed photographs,
whole albums to choose from and model ourselves
with and after, because it was night,
and whatever we made was going to have to diamond
both of us until morning. When I watched them pour
across the street it was like

3.

I wrote a story about my father, only
the first sentence was true. No knowing when I finished
and denying beginning both
lungs and bees engineer a peace not peace.
So when I tell you I don't know anything you can
believe me with skin, as the glitch
language is there to argue with truly
stuns me into something like night. I wrote a story about gulls,

only the word goodbye was true, an army of referees in

two languages, one for winter and the other
for fall. A laughter filled the field designed to break people.
Silence for riding, the door to my bedroom would not
click shut, like silence the sun makes available in trees
and the desk trees are thin parable for.
The sun moved among my calculations
writing a story about a father stitched with bees.
I am standing by the sea, a parking lot for

4.

We had this ashtray
storing sex in a little annex. Without knowing
who had filled it (you and I had not and our fathers
had only just arrived) the guess I hazarded that afternoon
seemed to helium whole neighborhoods

against our chimes.
You suggested we play a game about celebrities.
In one round each person could use a word
and in the next rounds we couldn't use words.
We pasted cards to our foreheads and when our fathers
leaned in to hear us hazard our guesses
whole instants came to last like cigarettes.

At the breakfast table we averaged two blessings per meal
and conversation often lighted on as many
as six saints, one being baseball, another our house, another
the animal we had forgotten, another photographs,
another gulls eating ash from our hands to

5.

The horse melts to houses where her hooves touched water
so still its houses touch fire.
Air the masterpiece of obstruction, in color and
newly remastered
every night of our lives, an anniversary cleaning its teeth with gulls.
We can agree gulls are as much a government as the changing
of sails, but by what color rope? The horse says governments
speak in color bars while television
only speaks in news.

In my father's version news is spun from trees' fingers
as peace stained blue
and you and I need it clear. The meteorologist perched above the
sea setting off flares incites us to
move, but you select the sounds you bead yourself on.
You've fallen asleep in the lighthouse again. I'll keep
listening for both of us tonight, rattling in the branches
lit red yellow blue

THE APPLE'S FLOOR

The age is not torturing he who am atomized by your embrace.

People die in things we don't even think of today, like castles.

A warning peace cruises softly over the public.

This truthful circuit. You're in my house how.

Directions exit directions, God following their slack.

Suffering is exhaling when one can't exit my music.

Hearing to music at maximum volume can cause a person to be death.

Throw another rose on the singer. Does he absorb?

The audience laughing in an orb.

December breaks onto the coast.

I'm so looking forward to becoming an environment in which some
creature occurs.

But I'm diagonal, day's mezzanines collapse.

Until the public passes into the twelve-hour tunnel burrowed between
these thumbs who crush crime.

I ride three modes to work: one underground, another with sunrise, the
last a passing cage.

Opera blasting from a passenger's buds.

When I arrived my student relayed the following.

"A Shakespearean actor breaks down in the face of a greenscreen.

His dialogue outsourced to plastic elves."

Who speaks into flat forest?

The echo has nowhere to go and go.

The second call its first dimension.

Above all I've endeavored to change my birth's location.

My parents the thing that's happened all week. Their warming rays a pile
of sleep.

He didn't have adults in his voice, though he was weeping with it.

I was trying to persuade this look of glass with a score in sand.

His parents in the vicinity waiting for a legal team on the beach.

They are there to tell what has happened actually.

By actual I mean verifiable, evidence printed in the world.

The train's window going live in daylight.

Its blade and geometric spray.

I wanted a surface to reflect its emissions.

And for all mouths who came to bathe there crippled with braces, foul
 fuel erased inside.

Each meal a heavy metal pool.

For a couple of years I up and died.

There's a reason you're reading this in black.

My ass is splashed with Mozart.

A lit candle saws his head off in the forest.

It is part of his practice. And things feel slightly alive.

Above a station in the metro someone executed two officers.

The New Year arrived and arrived.

My friends are here.

The papers said when the slayer exited his train we all spilled out, faces
 on an infinite bough.

The tear is ripped as a golden goblet from its body's bag.

Things feel a little alive.

"Sucking the sherbets, crooning the tunes," is part of the last line of John Ashbery's "Hop O' My Thumb." The quoted lines in "A Northist" are from Jessica Laser, in conversation. "This shirt is how I feel" is from Alice Notley's "At Night the States." The phrases "A Rubber Lion" and "Crescent Sun" are from the notebooks of Jean-Michel Basquiat.

.

Thank you Sara Akant, Rawaan Alkhatib, Micah Bateman, Katie Fowley, James Galvin, Callie Garnett, David Gorin, Gillian Olivia Blythe Hamel, Cathy Hong, Richard Kenney, Joe Kloc, Jessica Laser, Ben Lerner, Mark Levine, Eric Linsker, James Longley, Wendy Lotterman, Chris Martin, Ted Mathys, Andrés Millan, Jennifer Moxley, Jeff Nagy, Hilary Plum, Geoffrey G. O'Brien, Adrienne Raphel, Margaret Ross, Zach Savich, Robyn Schiff, Christian Schlegel, Rob Schlegel, Mary Austin Speaker, Colby Sommerville, Cole Swensen, Bridget Talone, Gotaro Toda, Mónica de la Torre, Alex Walton, and Lisa Wells. My gratitude also to Sarah Heidt, Perry Lentz, and G. C. Waldrep for foundational generosity and wisdom.

Thank you to the Iowa Writers' Workshop, the MacDowell Colony, Yaddo, the International Institute of Modern Letters at Victoria University (New Zealand), the Norton Island Residency, my friends and family who hosted me while I wrote, and Omnidawn for time and support.

Thank you to the editors of the following journals, where some of these poems first appeared: *Bat City Review*, *BOMB*, *The Claudius App*, *Colorado Review*, *Denver Quarterly*, *The Fanzine*, *Fence*, *Granta*, *Handsome*, *Hyperallergic*, *The New Republic*, *OmniVerse*, the *Petri Press* blog, *Strange Cage*, *The Volta*, and *WIDMA*. "Antibody" was featured as a broadside for the Fort Gondo reading series in St. Louis, Missouri.

All my love to my family.

photo: Charlotte McCurdy

Daniel Poppick's work has been recognized with fellowships from Yaddo, the MacDowell Colony, and the Iowa Writers' Workshop, where he earned his MFA in 2011. A graduate of Kenyon College, he has taught writing and literature at SUNY Purchase College, Coe College, Victoria University (New Zealand), and the University of Iowa. He lives in Brooklyn, where he co-edits the Catenary Press.

The Police
Daniel Poppick

Cover photo courtesy of the author.

Cover and interior text set in Didot, Futura Std, and Joanna MT Std

Cover and interior design by Gillian Olivia Blythe Hamel

Publication of this book was made possible in part by gifts from:
The New Place Fund
Robin & Curt Caton

Omnidawn Publishing
Oakland, California
2017

Rusty Morrison & Ken Keegan, senior editors & co-publishers
Gillian Olivia Blythe Hamel, managing editor
Cassandra Smith, poetry editor & book designer
Sharon Zetter, poetry editor, book designer & development officer
Liza Flum, poetry editor & marketing assistant
Peter Burghardt, poetry editor
Juliana Paslay, fiction editor
Gail Aronson, fiction editor
Cameron Stuart, marketing assistant
Avren Keating, administrative assistant
Kevin Peters, OmniVerse Lit Scene editor
Sara Burant, OmniVerse reviews editor
Josie Gallup, publicity assistant
SD Sumner, copyeditor
Briana Swain, marketing assistant